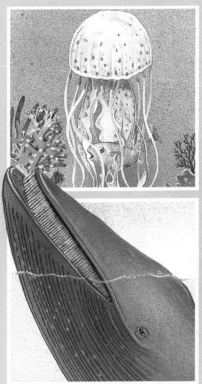

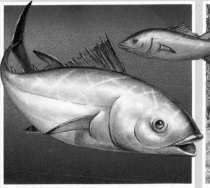

TABLE OF CONTENTS

SEAS AND OCEANS 7

SEA ANIMALS 55

FRAGILE OCEANS 95

ADVENTURES AT SEA 115

Translation:
Lara M. Andahazy

IMAGES
The Seas

Concept:
Émilie Beaumont

Text:
M. R. Pimont

Illustrations:
F. Guiraud, F. Ruyer, Y. Lequesne

FLEURUS

SEAS AND OCEANS

THE FIRST OCEAN

When Earth was new, there were no oceans. The first ocean appeared millions of years after the earth was formed.

At first, Earth was covered with volcanoes. It was also bombarded with giant rocks from outer space.

Little by little, Earth cooled down and the water vapor spit out by the volcanoes changed into water. This took millions of years.

THE EARTH MOVES

After the earth was formed, its crust cracked.
Huge plates were formed and started to move.

Look closely at these four pictures. They show where the land was on our planet and how it moved over millions of years.

This is how our planet looks today.

Even now, millions of years later, these plates are still moving.
The earth shakes when they bump into each other.

THE FIRST SIGNS OF LIFE

These odd creatures were among the first animals to appear in the oceans. They had tentacles but no eyes or mouths.

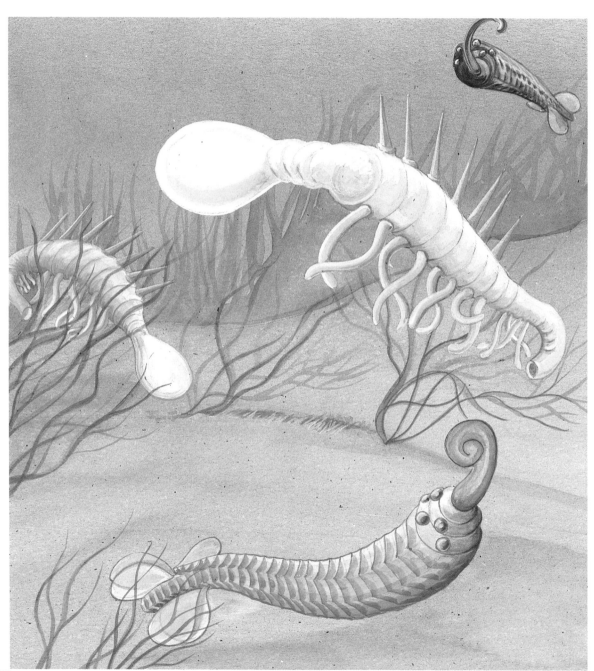

THE FIRST SHELLFISH—AMMONITES

Ammonites appeared 400 million years ago—well before the dinosaurs. They disappeared when the dinosaurs did.

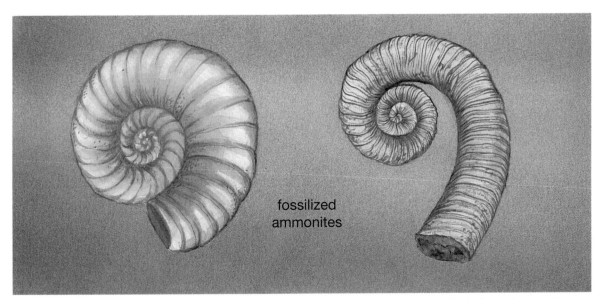

fossilized
ammonites

Ammonites' shells had compartments filled with air which let them float.

nautilus

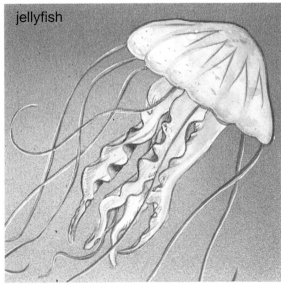

jellyfish

The nautilus is a cousin of the ammonites. Nautiluses still exist today. Sharks love to eat them. Jellyfish existed at the same time as ammonites.

THE FIRST ANIMALS TO HAVE SHELLS

These early animals were small. Some looked like plants.
They lived among sponges and coral.

1–Sea lily: this animal is the ancestor of starfish and sea urchins.
2–Trilobites: they were the ancestors of crabs and lobsters.

THE FIRST FISH

The bodies and heads of the first fish were covered with armor.
Some did not have jaws, just round holes for mouths.

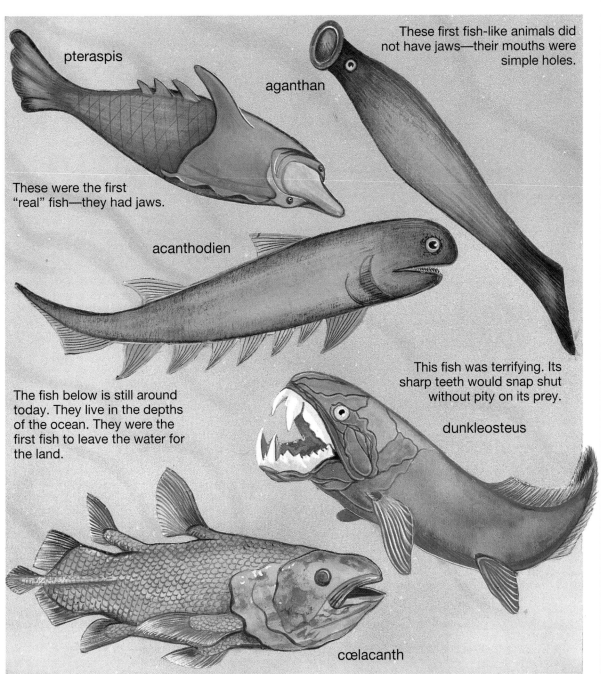

pteraspis

aganthan

These first fish-like animals did not have jaws—their mouths were simple holes.

These were the first "real" fish—they had jaws.

acanthodien

This fish was terrifying. Its sharp teeth would snap shut without pity on its prey.

dunkleosteus

The fish below is still around today. They live in the depths of the ocean. They were the first fish to leave the water for the land.

cœlacanth

IN THE AGE OF THE DINOSAURS

Huge, strange animals lived in the oceans while the dinosaurs walked the earth.

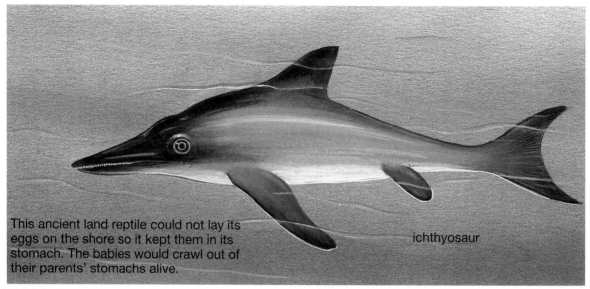

This ancient land reptile could not lay its eggs on the shore so it kept them in its stomach. The babies would crawl out of their parents' stomachs alive.

ichthyosaur

This animal's ancestors lived on land. Their eyes were as big as your head.

One of his children might haunt Loch Ness to this day!

plesiosaurus

This sea monster caught fish thanks to its long neck. When it was on land, it walked on its four fins.

THEY LEFT THE OCEANS

The first birds came out of the oceans. They did not have any feathers on their wings and they had sharp teeth to bite with!

pterodactyl

This bird could not land on the ground. It would grab onto trees and hang like a bat.

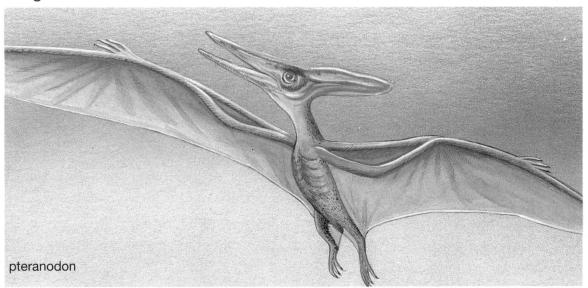

pteranodon

This monster glided through the air while looking for fish. All these birds have disappeared, just like the dinosaurs.

CAN YOU FIND ME?

Listen carefully to the descriptions of each animal and point out each one on the picture below. 1. I sleep like a bat. 2. I have huge eyes.

3. Strong armor protects me. 4. I use my fins to walk when I leave the water. 5. I was the first shellfish but I disappeared with the dinosaurs.

THE SEAS AND OCEANS OF PLANET EARTH

Astronauts who have seen our planet from space say that it is blue—more of the planet's surface is covered with water than with land.

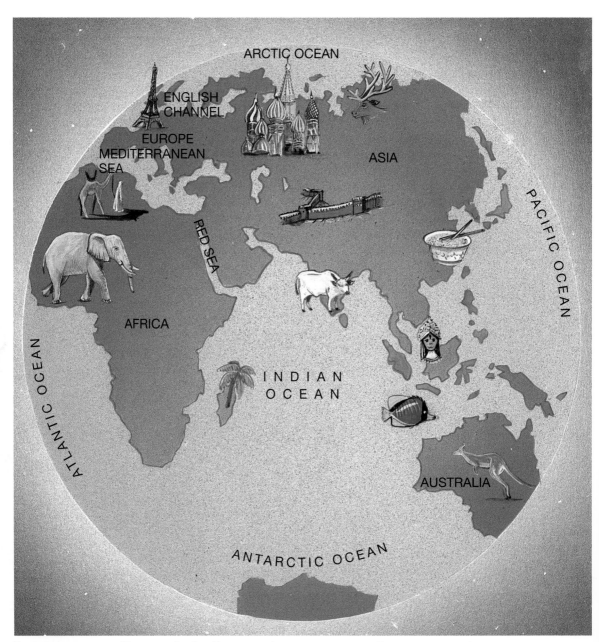

Seas are smaller and shallower than oceans. Some are almost completely surrounded by land.

Earth would be a dead planet if it were not for its seas and oceans because life began in them a very long time ago—around 3.5 billion years ago.

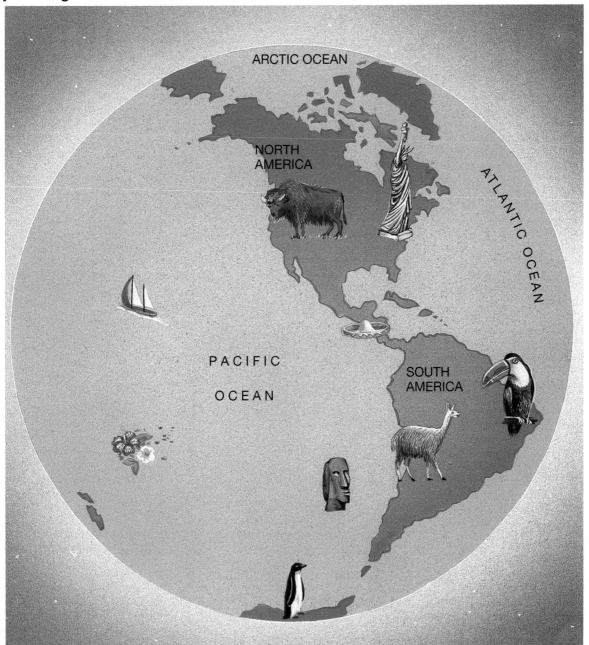

Oceans are huge bodies of constantly moving water. They can be many miles deep.

THE ATLANTIC OCEAN

A boat leaving Europe or Africa must cross the Atlantic ocean to get to the Americas.

1

New York

2

West Indies beach

3

Rio de Janeiro

4

Argentinean cowboy

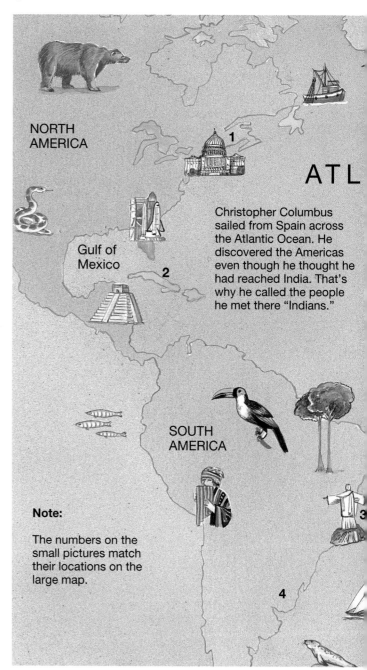

NORTH
AMERICA

ATL

Gulf of
Mexico

1

2

Christopher Columbus sailed from Spain across the Atlantic Ocean. He discovered the Americas even though he thought he had reached India. That's why he called the people he met there "Indians."

SOUTH
AMERICA

3

4

Note:

The numbers on the small pictures match their locations on the large map.

Children in Africa can swim in the Atlantic Ocean just like children in Brazil can but they are thousands of miles apart!

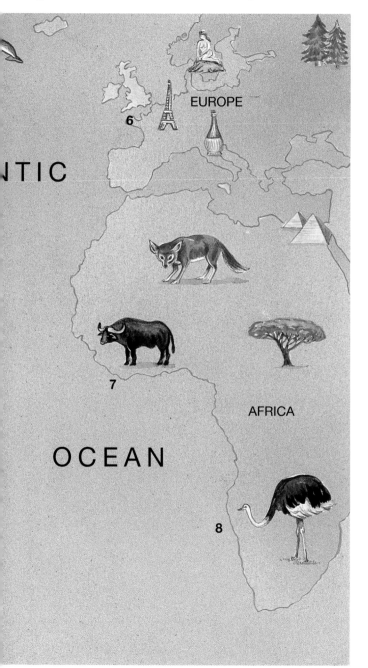

EUROPE

ATLANTIC

AFRICA

OCEAN

countryside in Greenland

small port in Brittany

Abidjan

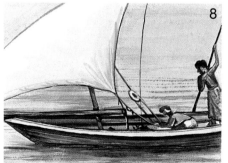

fisherman off the coast of Africa

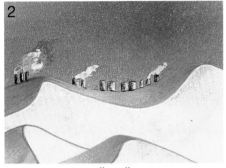
bottom of the Red Sea

oil well

Seychelles island beach

Madagascar landscape

THE INDIAN OCEAN

The African continent and many countries including India and Australia touch the edges of the Indian Ocean.

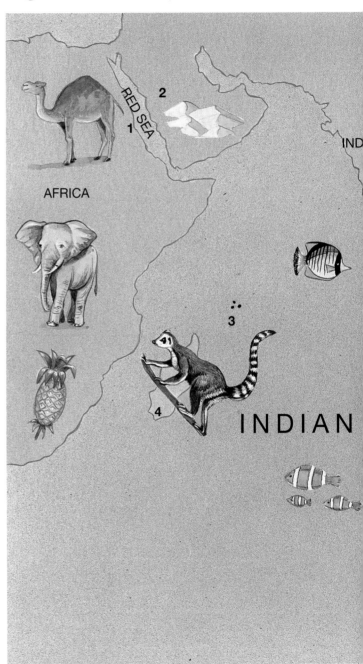

RED SEA

AFRICA

IND

INDIAN

Terrible cyclones are born over the Indian Ocean. The winds carry heavy rains to land during the monsoon season.

CHINA

OCEAN

AUSTRALIA

Bengal tiger

an Indian riding an elephant

orangutan in Malaysia

Australian aborigine

1

Mount Fuji

2

rice paddy in China

3

beach

4

Australian desert

THE PACIFIC OCEAN

China, Japan and Australia are on one side of the Pacific Ocean; North and South America are on the other.

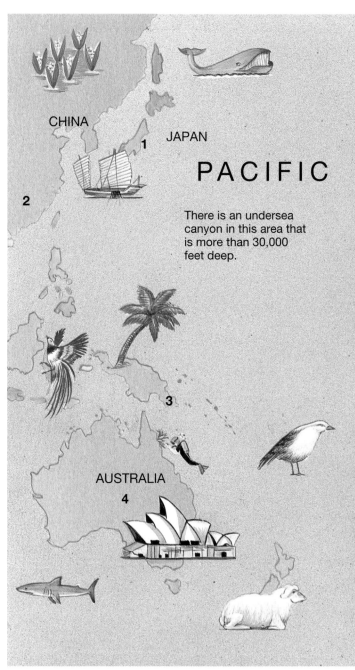

CHINA

JAPAN

1

2

PACIFIC

There is an undersea canyon in this area that is more than 30,000 feet deep.

3

AUSTRALIA

4

It is the widest and deepest of all the oceans. You could fit all the land on the planet into it.

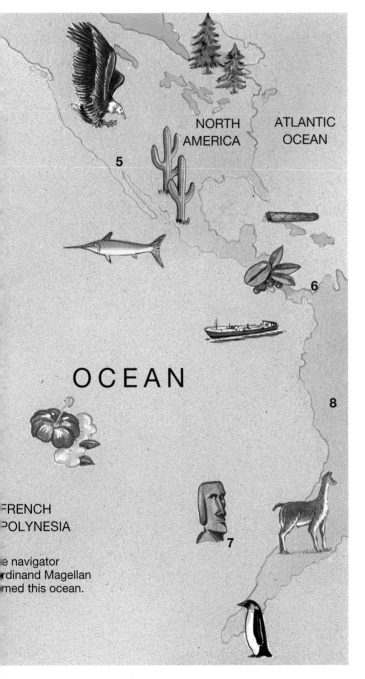

NORTH
AMERICA

ATLANTIC
OCEAN

5

OCEAN

6

8

FRENCH
POLYNESIA

7

e navigator
rdinand Magellan
med this ocean.

San Francisco's Golden Gate Bridge

Panama Canal

statues on Easter Island

Bolivian fisherman

POLAR OCEANS

These oceans can be found at the North and South Poles. They freeze over in winter—a thick layer of ice, an ice floe, covers them.

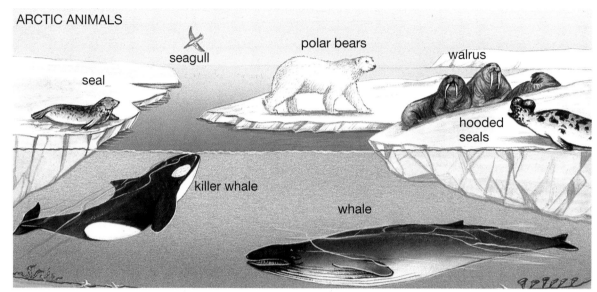

ARCTIC ANIMALS

seagull

polar bears

walrus

seal

hooded seals

killer whale

whale

The Arctic Ocean is full of animals in the summer because food—millions of shrimp—is plentiful.

ANTARCTIC ANIMALS

sea elephant

sea lion

penguins

seal

leopard seal

squid

During the summer, large icebergs that broke off of the glaciers melt and add lots of fresh water to the ocean.

Thousands of new icebergs appear in the polar oceans every year. These huge blocks of fresh water float on the sea.

Glaciers slide little by little towards the sea. Blocks break off—these are icebergs. It takes 2 to 4 years for an iceberg to melt.

Huge icebergs break off the sheet of ice at the South Pole. The largest ever seen from an airplane was almost 220 miles long! Penguins live on these icebergs.

Penguins are the best-known Antarctic (South Pole) animals. These birds can not fly but they can swim very, very fast.

27

THE MEDITERRANEAN SEA

The water in the Mediterranean Sea comes from the Atlantic Ocean. Some drops of water travel for 100 years before returning to the ocean.

"Mediterranean" means "between land." This sea is almost completely surrounded. Its water is saltier than the water in the Atlantic.

small port in Corsica

Tunisian landscape

Many ports welcome fishing and tourist boats. Mountains often stand tall close to the shore.

The Mediterranean sea bottom is home to many different fish.
Some can not be found anywhere else.

blue fin tuna

black grouper

sar

red angler fish

small castagnoles

Mediterranean rosefish

THE DEAD SEA

This sea is called the "Dead Sea" because it is so salty that fish can not live in it. It is dark at only 36 feet deep!

The Dead Sea is in the middle of a desert. It is a tiny sea that looks like a large lake.

Strange salt sculptures rise up out of the water in shallow areas. You do not need to know how to swim here—everyone floats without even trying!

THE RED SEA

This narrow sea got its name because the algae that live in it turn red when they die.

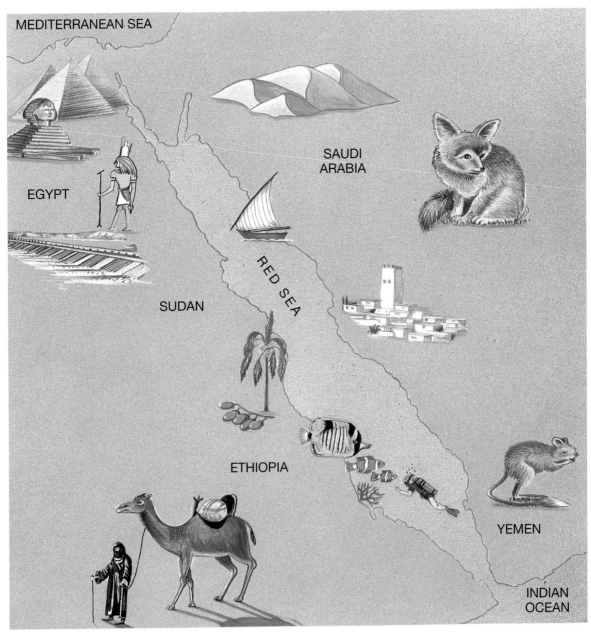

MEDITERRANEAN SEA

SAUDI ARABIA

EGYPT

RED SEA

SUDAN

ETHIOPIA

YEMEN

INDIAN OCEAN

Lots of scuba divers visit the Red Sea. The fish get used to them and swim close to have their pictures taken!

ROCK BUILDERS

The very pretty "rocks" called coral that can be found in warm waters are not really rocks. They are colonies of tiny animals.

Each animal has a mouth that is surrounded by several arms. When they are hungry they stretch their arms out of their shells and catch microscopic crabs.

These animals need to protect themselves. To do so they build a very solid "shell" around themselves. Their shells, pressed close together, make funny-shaped "rocks" of different sizes. Not all corals make rocks; some look like beautiful plants.

Some coral reefs are very long and form barriers along the coast that can be several miles long.

coral reef

Coral reefs are one of the most beautiful things that nature can make. They are mostly found in the Pacific Ocean.

LIFE IN A CORAL REEF

The longest coral reef lies off the shore of Australia.
A multitude of colorful fish live and eat there.

THE GALAPAGOS ISLANDS

The Galapagos Islands are extinct volcanoes.
Plant seeds sprouted on the cool lava flows.

This undersea volcano grew with every eruption. It became one of the volcanic islands in the Galapagos when it reached the surface.

a plant growing in cold lava

a Galapagos cormorant

The wind carried seeds to this deserted island and ships brought insects. Other animals and birds swam and flew to the island.

THE ANIMALS OF THE GALAPAGOS ISLANDS

The animals on the Galapagos Islands are not like those on the mainland. They are protected—no one can hunt them.

Iguanas are sea lizards— they like climbing and diving.

The shells of the turtles on each island are different from those on the other islands.

The blue-footed gannet lifts its webbed feet high in order to seduce its mate.

Galapagos crabs have left the ocean and live on the islands.

AT THE BOTTOM OF THE OCEANS

The ocean floor is made up of very different landscapes: mountains, plains, volcanoes, abrupt cliffs and more.

Some parts of the ocean floors are covered with volcanoes and cut by deep holes.

Most of the ocean floor is made up of great plains sprinkled in places with large rocks.

BIG "PILLOWS"

When burning lava from a volcano spills under water it makes large "pillows" that pile up on the bottom.

The surface of these "pillows" cools down quickly but they stay hot inside for a long time.

LIFE IN THE DEPTHS OF THE OCEANS

Sunlight can not reach the bottom of the ocean and yet animals live in the cold and the dark.

Sea lilies are animals that have been around for millions of years.

Fish in the depths of the oceans do not eat very often but they are able to swallow prey as big as they are.

HOT SPRINGS IN THE DEPTHS

Hot springs are like oases in the seas.
They provide food for many animals.

Huge red worms, large shellfish, sea anemones, crabs and giant squid
live near these hot springs.

TWO FISH OF THE DEPTHS

They have great big eyes to see the light given off by other animals in the dark. The bigger ones eat the smaller ones!

This fish has 350 tiny "lamps" that attract other fish. It swims with its mouth wide open in order to gobble up everything that goes by.

This fish is a real fisherman. It uses its luminous fishing-pole-shaped fin to attract small fish and swallows them whole.

WATER TRAVELS

The oceans' role is very important: they create the clouds which travel far and wide carrying water vapor to the land.

The sun heats up the ocean water. Water vapor rises and forms clouds. Wind pushes the clouds in the sky. When the air gets cold, tiny drops of vapor clump together and fall in the form of raindrops, hail or snowflakes. The water flows down the streams and rivers to the oceans... and it all starts over again!

CURRENTS

Currents are like rivers in the oceans. They carry great amounts of warm or cold water.

You can spot currents in the sea: they are a different color and they carry food that draws fish and birds.

These baby turtles are riding a current.

Currents can carry a bottle from Mexico to France!

WHERE DO WAVES COME FROM?

The wind creates waves when it blows on the sea. The waves then rush to shore and break against the beaches and rocks.

There is no wind on this beach and yet there are waves. They were born very far away in the middle of the ocean.

When it is really stormy, waves can get big enough to swallow up ships!

THE OCEAN MOVES TO AND FRO

The water climbs to its highest point on the beach at high tide.
At low tide, it recedes to its lowest point.

Water climbs up the beach for six hours. Worms, small crabs and fish come out of their hiding places to look for food.

Water recedes for the next six hours. Birds hunt for the worms and shellfish that stay in the moist sand and mud.

It is the moon that pulls the earth's water towards itself and causes the movement of the tides. Sometimes the sun lends a helping hand!

SUN

MOON

EARTH

Mont-Saint-Michel has the biggest tides in all Europe.

The biggest tides take place when the sun, the moon and the earth are in a line. The strength of the sun is added to the strength of the moon.

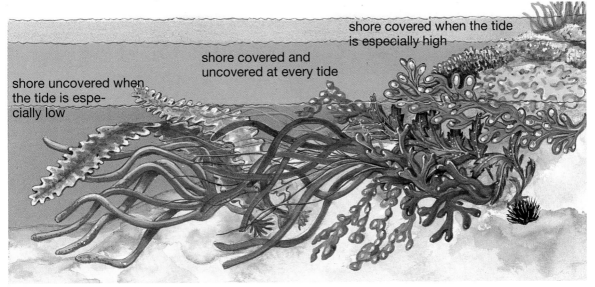

shore covered when the tide is especially high

shore covered and uncovered at every tide

shore uncovered when the tide is especially low

Algae choose the best place for themselves to grow on the shore. Some are always under water and others see the sun at low tide.

45

TIDAL WAVES!

Tidal waves do not come from the tides!
They are series of huge waves that flood the shore.

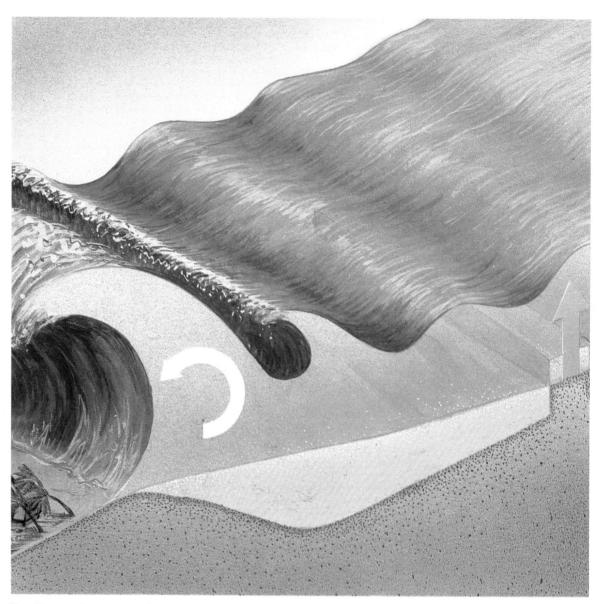

Earthquakes can happen at the bottom of the sea. Undersea volcanoes can erupt. When these things happen, whirlpools rise to the surface and huge waves race across the seas and tidal waves crash into the coast.

WHY IS THE WATER IN THE SEA SALTY?

Your eyes sting if you open them under sea water. And if you swallow some, you can taste the salt.

The hot water in the first oceans might have pulled the salt out of the rocks.

Sea salt is gathered in salt marshes.

Some seas have more salt than others. The Dead Sea is very salty.

THE STORY OF WAVES AND CLIFFS

Cliffs are very tall, very straight walls of rock. Waves whip against them and dig arches and caves in them.

Waves dig at the foot of a cliff first. Then they turn the rocks into pebbles.

Waves have dug an arch in this cliff.

When the roof of the arch falls...

a small island, an islet, is created!

FROM A ROCK TO A GRAIN OF SAND

Water worms its way into cracks in rocks near mountain tops. When the water freezes, it breaks the rocks and small pieces slip into streams.

These pieces of rock become smaller and smaller as they are carried by the streams and then the rivers to the sea.

If the tides gather these tiny pieces in one place they can form a barrier that will create a saltwater pond.

49

SAND SCULPTURES

Sand is found near the coast but not at sea! When it is dry it slips through your fingers. You can make sand castles out of it when it is wet.

The rising tide carries the sand to the top of the beaches. It stays there while the tide goes out. Then, the wind carries the grains of sand and piles them up in small hills called dunes.

Water moves grains little by little with the help of wind and currents. This makes miniature dunes that look like wrinkles in the sand.

FLOWERS AND ANIMALS IN THE DUNES

Plants hold the dunes in place when the wind blows. This is why you should not pick them. If you did, the dunes would be blown away.

DELTAS—NEITHER SEA NOR LAND

Rivers sometimes create dream-like landscapes when they reach the ocean. The beautiful Camargue is in the Rhone delta.

Rivers deposit mud, sand and gravel and build "earthen arms." The fresh water from the river mingles with salt water from the ocean between these arms.

Animals and plants of the river deltas of warm countries.

Guardians raise horses in the Camargue.

The guardians live in these cabins built on narrow strips of land.

TRICKY QUESTIONS!

These questions may look easy but watch out for tricks! You can find the answers on the pages you have just read and at the bottom of this one.

– 1 –
Is the water in the clouds salty?
YES or NO?
WHY?

– 2 –
Where were the first signs of life?
In the skies or in the oceans?

– 3 –
Name two fish that live in the Dead Sea.

– 4 –
Is coral:
a flower?
a rock?
an animal?

– 5 –
Are tides caused by:
the wind blowing on the sea?
the moon that pulls on the sea water?
currents?

– 6 –
Are whales fish or cetaceans?

1) No, because only water vapor leaves the sea, not the salt (pg. 41). 2) In the ocean (pg. 10). 3) Are you sure there are fish in the Dead Sea? (pg. 30). 4) An animal, yes indeed! (pg. 32). 5) The moon (pg. 45). 6) Cetaceans (pg. 84).

MYSTERIOUS GAMES

Why is it so easy to float in the Dead Sea? How does the imprint of a sea shell become a fossil?

3 quarts of fresh water

the egg falls

water + cooking salt (2 1/2 cups)

the egg floats

EXPERIMENT

Imagine that the egg is a person and that the water in the bowl is the Dead Sea! The person floats.

Boil the water and the cooking salt so that they are completely mixed together. Let the water cool down before trying this experiment.

thick layer of modeling clay

seashell

small cardboard box

liquid plaster

after it has hardened:

print

MAKE A FOSSIL

Push a seashell firmly into the modeling clay and then carefully take it out. Pour the liquid plaster into the print. Once the plaster hardens you will have a plaster "fossil." True fossils are not filled with plaster but with sand!

SEA ANIMALS

CRABS

Look for baby crabs among the rocks at low tide. Did you know that they will leave their shells when they are too small?

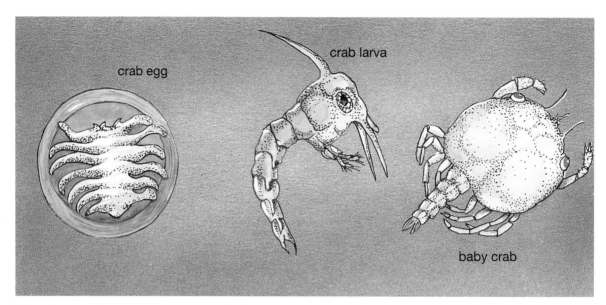

crab egg

crab larva

baby crab

The larva that comes out of the egg uses its tiny legs to swim. It will change shape six times before making its first shell.

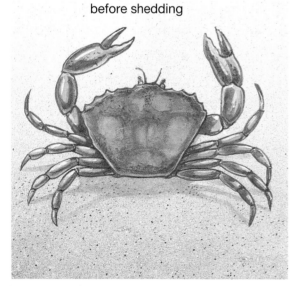

before shedding

after shedding

old shell

Crabs drink lots of water in order to leave their shells. The water makes their bodies swell and break their shells! At first, their new shells are soft.

SAND FLEAS

Sand fleas are the cousins of crabs because they have shells.
They are crustaceans the size of a fingernail!

Sand fleas do not like the light. They hide in the sand during the day.
At night they come out and nibble on seaweed.

Baby sand fleas know how to jump when they come out of their eggs.
They quickly learn how to hide in the sand and how to swim!

BABY SOLES EYES CHANGE PLACES!

The larva that hatch out of mother sole's eggs look like the larva of other fish. But they will flatten out.

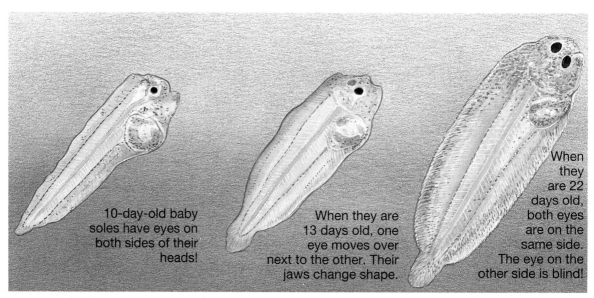

10-day-old baby soles have eyes on both sides of their heads!

When they are 13 days old, one eye moves over next to the other. Their jaws change shape.

When they are 22 days old, both eyes are on the same side. The eye on the other side is blind!

When the baby sole's two eyes are on the same side of its head, it leaves the spot where it was born and goes to the bottom of the sea.

Soles are flat fish that can be up to 25 inches long. They spend their time hidden in the sand and gravel on the sea floor.

SEAHORSE SUPER DAD

These odd fish have horse heads and the father carries the eggs. He gives birth to about a hundred babies.

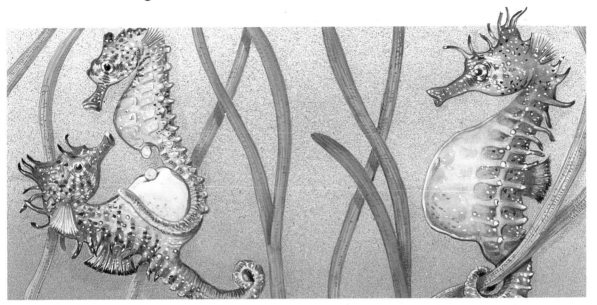

Mother seahorse places her eggs in the father's pouch.

One month later, the eggs hatch in the father's swollen pouch.

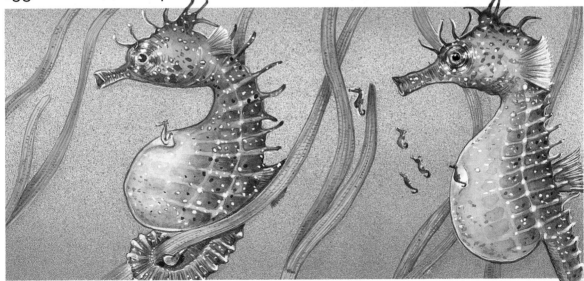

Father shakes his pouch while hanging on to seaweed and out pops a baby!

The baby seahorses come out five at a time during one whole day or maybe even two.

BABY DOLPHINS HAVE GODMOTHERS

Dolphins are not fish. They have lungs that fill with air through a hole on the top of their heads called the blow hole.

the godmother is keeping watch

Baby dolphins grow in their mothers stomachs for a whole year before coming out tail first. The godmother makes sure the birth goes well.

The mother pushes her baby to the surface so it can breathe. The godmother drives away sharks by hitting them hard with her nose.

THE BABIES OF THE GIANT TURTLES

The leatherback turtle lives in deep warm waters. The mothers climb onto land once a year to lay their eggs.

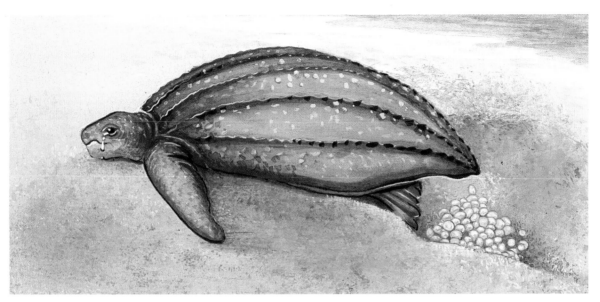

The mother leatherback turtle digs a hole in the sand and lays close to a hundred eggs in it. Then she buries them and goes back to the sea.

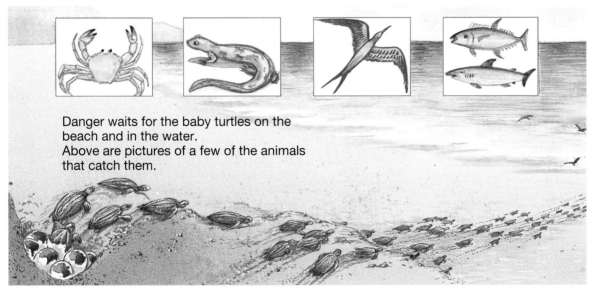

Danger waits for the baby turtles on the beach and in the water.
Above are pictures of a few of the animals that catch them.

Seven weeks later, the baby turtles leave their eggs and go to the sea where they will grow into giant leatherback turtles.

PENGUINS OF THE SOUTH POLE

Penguins are birds but they can not fly. They can swim very well though. They live on the ice and in the very cold ocean.

Mama penguins place their eggs between the feet of the fathers and go fishing. The fathers stand still and do not eat until the mothers come back.

The mothers return when the babies are born. The mothers then watch over the babies while the skinny fathers rush off to feast on fish.

A FEW SEA BIRDS

Some live on the shores. Others spend all their time flying above the oceans and only go to land to reproduce.

Albatrosses are large birds that mate for life. Both parents help raise their children. This father has brought food back for his children.

Cormorants dive underwater to catch fish.

Puffins look a bit like clowns and love to eat small herrings.

SEA AND RIVER TRAVELERS

Salmon find their way by tasting and smelling the water in the rivers where they are born and in which they swim.

salmon eggs

small alevin with its sack of egg yolk

alevin that lives in the river for two years

young salmon

The alevin that comes out of the egg will slowly grow into a young salmon able to take a long trip in the ocean.

Adult salmon leave the sea. They swim up their rivers to where the females lay their eggs. The adventure starts all over again!

3,750 MILES ACROSS THE ATLANTIC!

Eels are born in the Sargasso Sea near North America and grow up in a river in Europe before returning to the ocean.

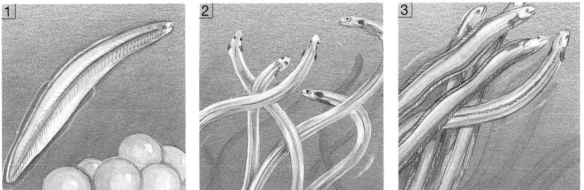

1 – Larvae come out of their eggs in the Sargasso Sea. The current carries them away.
2 – Larvae become elvers (young eels) when they are three years old. 3 – They swim up river.

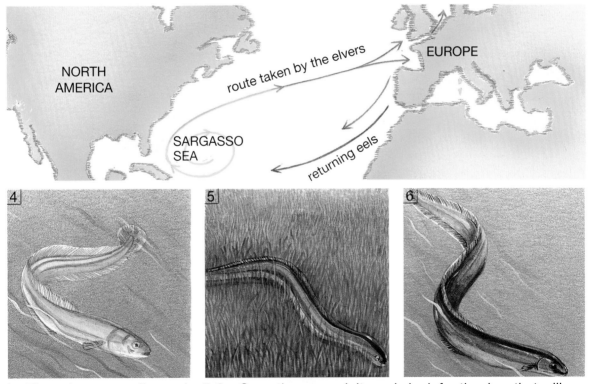

4 – Elvers become yellow eels. 5-6 – Once they are adults, eels look for the river that will carry them back to the ocean. They cross the ocean to the Sargasso Sea where they lay their eggs.

AN OYSTER LUNCH FOR THIS STARFISH

Starfish are headless animals. They move around using the suction cups on their arms. They can grow new arms if they lose one!

Starfish's mouths are on their stomachs, pointed towards the ground. If put on their backs—they will have a very hard time turning over.

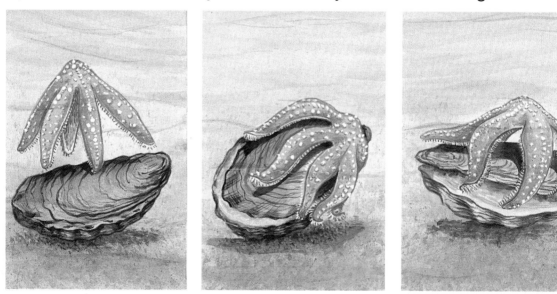

The starfish spreads apart the two halves of the oyster's shell, slips its stomach inside the shell, eats the oyster and pulls its stomach back out!

SEA URCHINS NIBBLE SEAWEED

You might find beautiful round shells tossed ashore by the sea on the beach. They are sea urchins' skeletons called "tests."

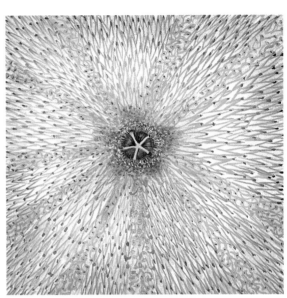

You can see the mouth and five teeth that the sea urchin uses to pull seaweed off of rocks in the middle of its stomach on the close-up picture.

Some sea urchins can dig holes in rocks to hide in.

Sea urchins' spines do not protect them from sea snails.

A SANDY LUNCH FOR THE COCKLE AND THE RAZOR CLAM

These shellfish hide in the sand. Their shells are made up of two halves. They sometimes push two odd tubes called siphons to the surface.

The cockle wiggles its strong foot to dig its way into the sand.

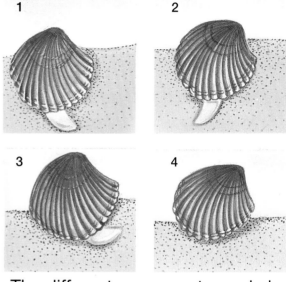

The different movements made by the cockle to get out of the sand.

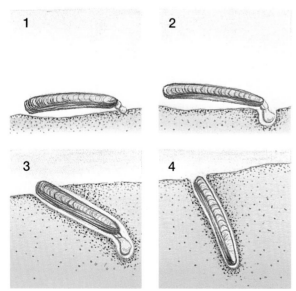

Razor clams can hide under up to three feet of sand.

Water goes in one siphon and comes out the other.

siphons

Razor clams filter water to find their food.

SCALLOPS

Scallops look around them with a hundred or so little blue eyes while the lower half of their shells is buried in the sand.

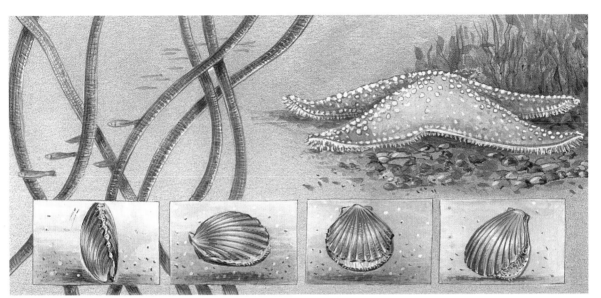

Scallops hop quickly away from starfish by snapping the two halves of their shells rapidly open and shut.

Scallops can easily spot danger thanks to their many eyes and tentacles.

SNAILS' COUSINS

These shellfish crawl with one foot and suck up mollusks with a trunk or nibble on seaweed with a rough tongue.

The murex burns holes in shellfish with acid and sucks out the flesh.

The whelk loves to eat oysters. It breaks open their shells.

The limpet leaves an odorous mark behind so it can find its spot again.

Winkles close a tiny door in their shells, the operculum, at low tide.

CLEVER FISH

Some fish have very clever tricks to catch worms, crustaceans and even other small fish!

Mullets search the sea floor with their two barbels.

Angler fish use their filaments like fishing poles.

Moray eels hide in cracks and wait for their prey to go by.

Scorpion fish sting their prey with their poisonous stingers.

A CLEAN-UP FISH

Labroids set up "cleaning stations."
Their clients, other fish, wait in line for their turn.

Labroids eat away the sick flesh on other fish as well as small crustaceans that cling to their skin and bother them.

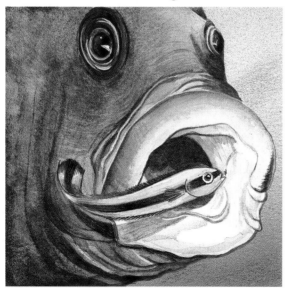

A tiny labroid is cleaning the mouth of a big grouper.

This shark is wandering around with its own clean-up fish.

WHAT DO SHARKS EAT?

These scary-looking fish have jaws lined with several rows of teeth.
Whenever a tooth falls out another grows in.

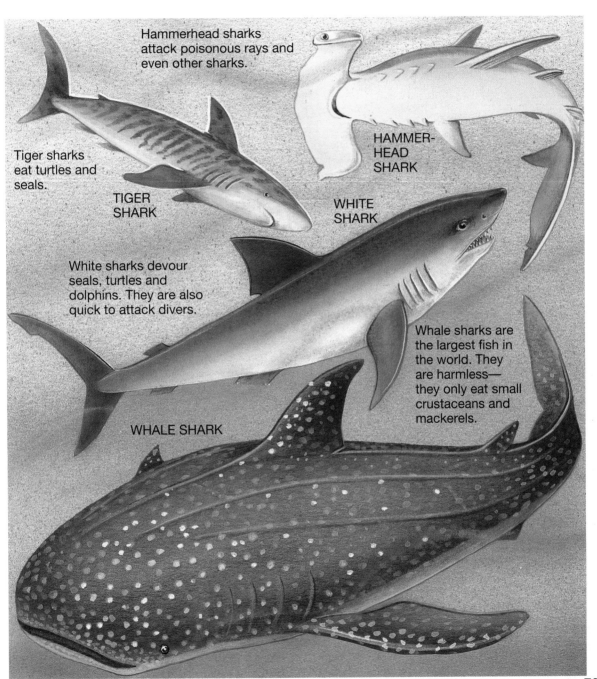

Hammerhead sharks
attack poisonous rays and
even other sharks.

HAMMER-
HEAD
SHARK

Tiger sharks
eat turtles and
seals.

TIGER
SHARK

WHITE
SHARK

White sharks devour
seals, turtles and
dolphins. They are also
quick to attack divers.

Whale sharks are
the largest fish in
the world. They
are harmless—
they only eat small
crustaceans and
mackerels.

WHALE SHARK

SEA SOUP—PLANKTON

Plankton is the main source of food for giant whales.
Mussels, small fish and certain sea birds also love to eat plankton!

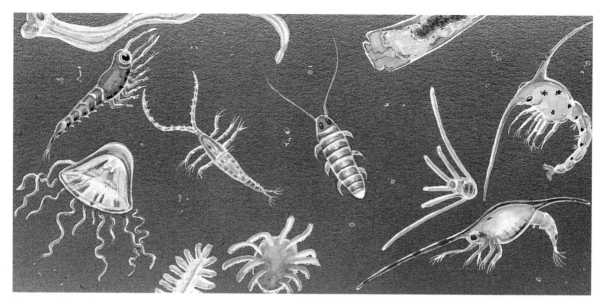

Plankton is made up of tiny algae, as well as eggs, larvae and other animals smaller than your fingernail!

baleen

Whale baleen looks like the teeth of a comb. Whales filter water with their baleen and keep the plankton to eat.

BABY SEALS

Life is very difficult on the ice floe. Baby seals have to grow quickly and learn to catch fish by themselves in order to survive.

Baby seals are covered with long fur when they are born.

Their fur changes shortly after they are born. They continue to suckle.

Mother is gone. This baby seal hesitates a little before jumping into the water. He will soon learn to dive and catch crustaceans.

SEA STINGERS: JELLYFISH

If you see a pretty jellyfish floating in the waves, do not touch it—it will sting you with its poisonous stingers.

Jellyfish swim by contracting and releasing their bell-shaped umbrellas when they are not just floating.

jellyfish on the beach

Jellyfishs' mouths are found under their umbrellas. Their filament stingers bring food (shrimp, small crabs and tiny fish) to their mouths.

FROM PLANKTON TO KILLER WHALES

Below is a food chain—smaller animals get eaten by bigger animals!
What if plankton disappeared? Can you guess what would happen?!

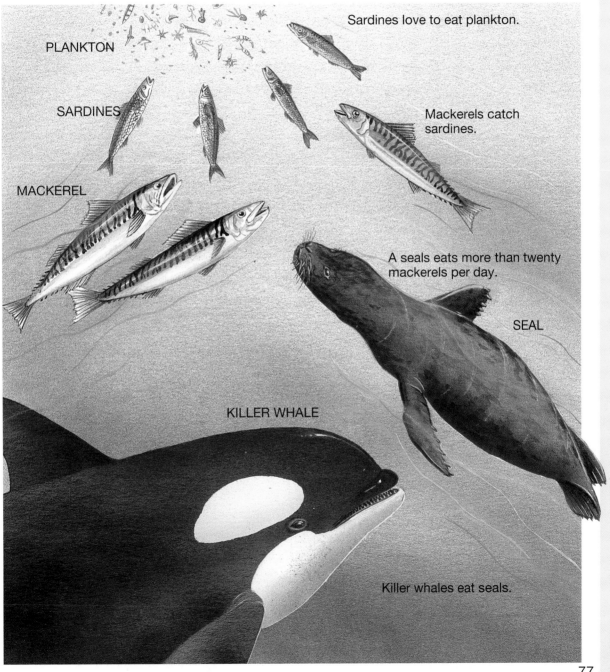

PLANKTON

Sardines love to eat plankton.

SARDINES

Mackerels catch
sardines.

MACKEREL

A seals eats more than twenty
mackerels per day.

SEAL

KILLER WHALE

Killer whales eat seals.

A PRAWN AND HIS FRIEND THE GOBY

Prawns dig dens in the mud. They only come out to capture food and only when it is safe to do so!

A small fish, the goby, stands guard. To thank it, the prawn lets it shelter in its den whenever an enemy is near.

Here is a huge conger eel! The goby hurries into the tunnel. The prawn knows that it is not safe to go out.

THE SEA ANEMONE AND THE CLOWN FISH

As soon as a fish or crustacean brushes against its tentacles, the sea anemone injects it with poison and swallows it up in its sac-like mouth.

This sea anemone has just captured a shrimp.

Small but clever, the clown fish rubs against the tentacles to cover itself with their smell. Its sea anemone will recognize it.

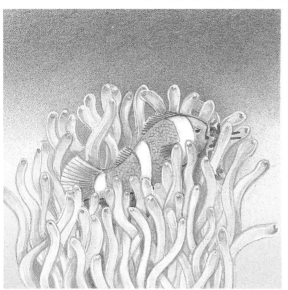

Safe from its enemies, the clown fish cleans up—after the anemone's meal, it gobbles up the crumbs that fall between the tentacles.

THE HERMIT CRAB'S TRICK

In order to protect its soft body, this crustacean takes over an empty shell or kicks an unfortunate animal out of its shell!

But the hermit crab grows and its shell gets too small! It has to move out and find a more comfortable house.

Sea anemones eat hermit crabs' enemies... and share their leftovers. The hermit crab will take the anemone with it when it moves!

CUTTLEFISH AND OCTOPUSES HAVE TRICKS TOO!

Buried under the sand, these huge mollusks have excellent eyes and spot their prey quickly, even in the dark.

cuttlefish bone

Cuttlefish take on the color of the sea floor and then shoot a strong spurt of water on the sand to draw crustaceans out of their hiding places!

Octopuses spit out a cloud of ink that takes on the shape of their bodies when they are scared. Their eggs hang from the ceiling of their caves.

SPONGES

Sponges are animals that do not have heads or mouths. Water leaves food behind as it moves through their holes and tunnels.

Sponges were thought to be plants for a long time. Above are a few different sizes and colors of sponges.

VERY ODD FISH

Flying fish and globe fish are funny! But watch out for the sawfish's teeth and the poisonous spines of the rock fish!

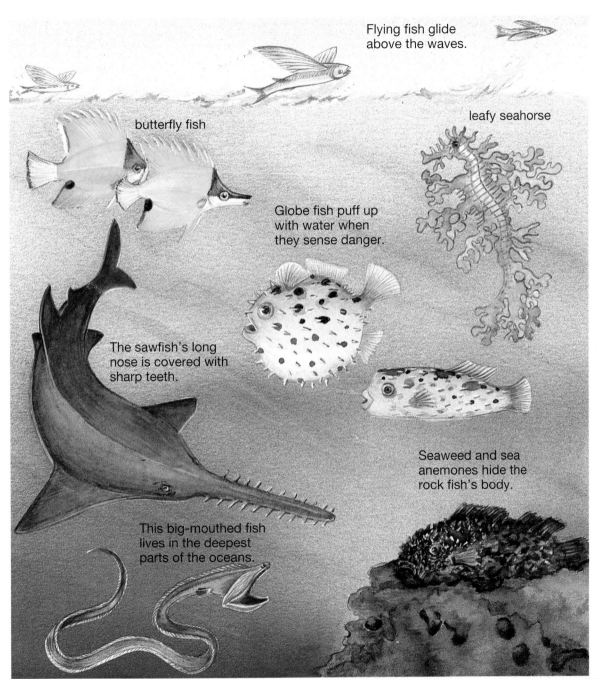

Flying fish glide above the waves.

butterfly fish

leafy seahorse

Globe fish puff up with water when they sense danger.

The sawfish's long nose is covered with sharp teeth.

Seaweed and sea anemones hide the rock fish's body.

This big-mouthed fish lives in the deepest parts of the oceans.

CETACEANS BREAK THE RECORDS

Whales are cetaceans that have baleen. Dolphins, sperm whales and narwhales are cetaceans that have teeth.

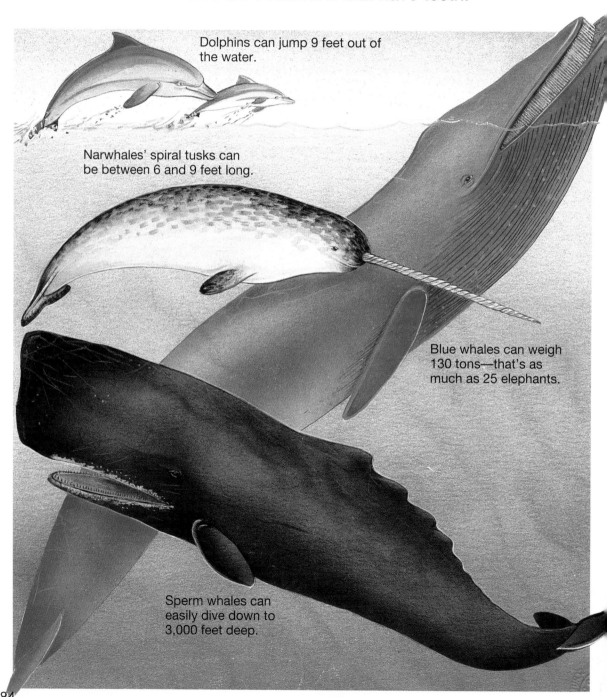

Dolphins can jump 9 feet out of the water.

Narwhales' spiral tusks can be between 6 and 9 feet long.

Blue whales can weigh 130 tons—that's as much as 25 elephants.

Sperm whales can easily dive down to 3,000 feet deep.

CHAMPION UNDERWATER FISHERMEN

Seals' cousins do not go fishing far from land so they learn to hunt for their prey deep under water.

Walruses can dive for 10 minutes and go down 240 feet deep.

Sea elephants dive 2,700 feet — almost as deep as sperm whales!

Seals can hold their breath for 40 minutes when they dive.

Clever sea lions dive quickly and bring back lobsters.

ALL PURPOSE PINCHERS

Crustaceans use their claws to eat with and also to walk, dig, scare others and fight!

When two male lobsters fight, the battle is often violent. The strongest one rips off its rival's claws and sometimes even kills and eats it.

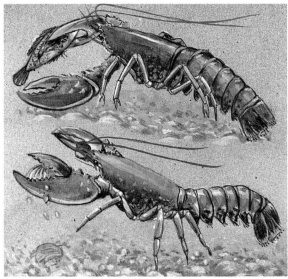

Lobsters walk on their claws. They rip off the flesh of fish with the small claw and crush shells with the big one.

BUILDING A HOME

Mollusk larvae build houses—their shells—in order to protect their soft bodies from the waves.

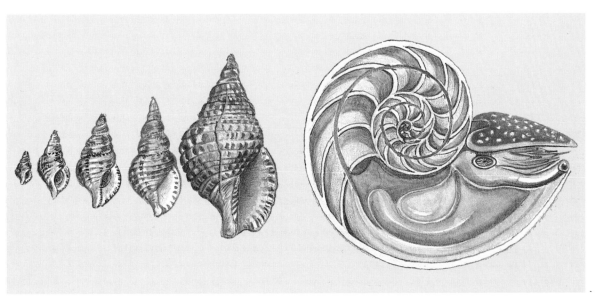

The shell grows as the animal grows.

Nautiluses live in the first room closest to the entrance.

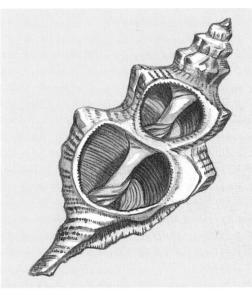

Find an empty spiral-shaped shell on the beach. Rub it very hard with sand paper to see the inside.

FISHING ON FOOT

Rocks and the beach are uncovered at low tide. This is the best time to go fishing with a bucket and a shrimping net.

FISHING FOR SHRIMP

Chose a puddle among the rocks. Scrape the bottom with your shrimping net from time to time. Pour the shrimp into your bucket.

HUNTING FOR GREEN CRABS

You can find them under rocks. Look at the picture of how to hold them so you won't get pinched. Don't forget to put the rocks back in place.

SHELLFISH AND SEA WORMS

You can eat your shellfish once they have been cooked.
The worms can be used as bait on a fishing hook.

Dig in the sand to find cockles while the sea is coming in.

You can find mussels and winkles clinging to rocks.

You can spot the worms' tunnels by looking for the tiny piles of sand they spit out. Dig deeply and grab the worms by the front.

TREASURE HUNT ON THE BEACH

Look at all the sea leaves behind on the beach when it recedes.
This is the "tide mark." It is full of wonderful things to collect!

How many of the following things can you find?
a sea urchin's test, a cuttlefish bone, cuttlefish eggs, a scallop
shell, a broken sea snail shell, seaweed, and a bird's feather.

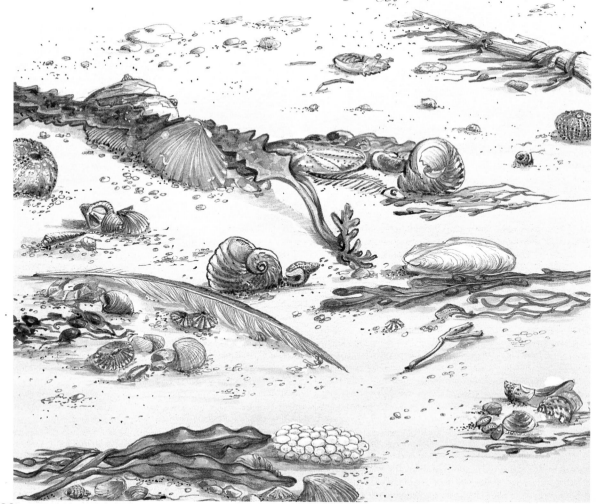

WHO EATS WHOM? WHO EATS WHAT?

Look closely at the picture and try to find what the animals listed below like to eat.

1) sardines. 2) a cuttlefish. 3) a starfish.
4) jellyfish. 5) winkles.

1) plankton. 2) a shrimp. 3) an oyster.
4) baby seahorses. 5) seaweed.

HIDE AND SEEK

Lots of animals are the same color as the sand or rocks.
Others have clever hiding places.

Can you find the all following animals?
sea anemones – a shrimp – a goby – a crab – a starfish – mussels –
whelk – a razor clam – limpets – an octopus – a sole – sand fleas –
a prawn

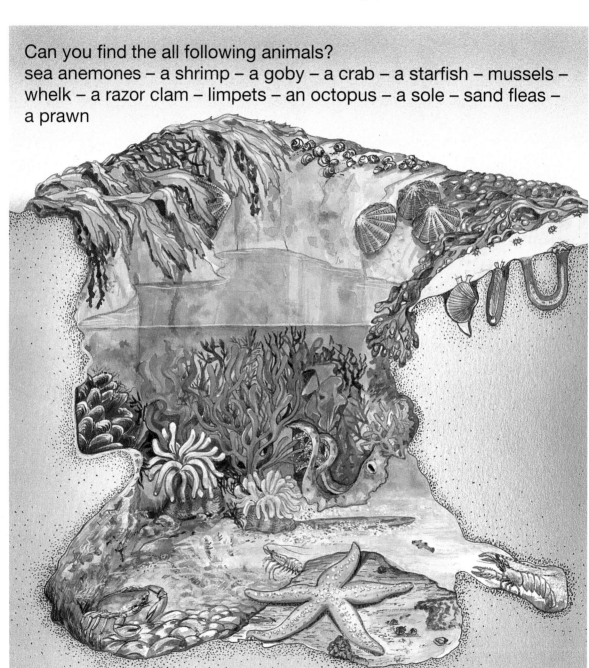

CAN YOU ANSWER THESE QUESTIONS?

If you do not know the answers, look back through the beginning of the book. Soon you will know the answers by heart!

Who has baleen? Who has teeth? Who has claws? Who breathes air at the surface? Who stings? Who sprays ink?

HEAD TO TAIL

We had to cut the pictures in two to invent these strange animals.
Can you match each head to its proper tail?

FRAGILE
OCEANS

FISHING TECHNIQUES AROUND THE WORLD

Men and women have always fished for food. In some countries they found very strange tactics!

This fisherman in Ceylon is perched on a post in the middle of the water.

Cormorants catch fish for this Chinese fisherman.

These fish are scared—they are surrounded by the inhabitants of this Pacific island! Dolphins drive whole schools of fish toward the nets.

ON A TRAWLER

Trawlers pull trawl nets behind them. These nets are shaped like giant pockets. They catch all the fish in their path.

The boat slows down while the fishermen lower the net. They will pull the net up with a winch when the net is full.

The fish are sorted and cleaned on the boat. Sometimes they are even frozen. Then the trawler brings its catch back to port. This is what it will sell to the fishmonger.

1 – Sole. 2 – Starfish. 3 – Cod. 4 – Monkfish. 5 – Hake.

TUNA FISHING

Have you ever eaten tuna? Fishermen go out to sea for several days on a large ship called a tuna boat in order to catch this fish.

The captain has spotted a school of fish! The fishermen attach sardines to their hooks. Streams of water that look like wiggling sardines spout out the sides of the boat at all times to attract the tuna. The tuna swim closer and fall into the trap.

PRAWNS, CRABS AND LOBSTERS

Fishermen store these crustaceans in big tanks of water on their boats so that they will stay alive until they reach the port.

crab and lobster pots

prawn pot

Fishermen put scraps of fish in cages called pots to attract these crustaceans. They drop the pots at the end of long chains to the sea bottom. A few hours later they pull them back up, empty out the crustaceans, put in new bait and start all over!

MUSSEL FARMS, OYSTER FARMS

Mussels and oysters are raised in farms. They open their shells to filter the sea water and keep the plankton.

These young mussels are attached to posts called "mussel beds." The mussel breeder will harvest them when they are nice and fat.

Oyster farmers lay oysters on sheets or long tubes of steel. They watch over them and protect them from starfish.

OYSTER PEARLS

Look at the mother-of-pearl lining of an oyster. If a grain of sand gets into the shell, the oyster will cover it in layers of mother-of-pearl!

Nuggets of mother-of-pearl are placed in oysters to cultivate pearls. They will be turned into pearls in three to five years!

These divers collect "black-lipped" pearl oysters that are cultivated in Tahiti. They contain beautiful black pearls.

OCEAN PLANTS

Algae are rootless plants. They are used as hiding places or even eaten by many sea animals.

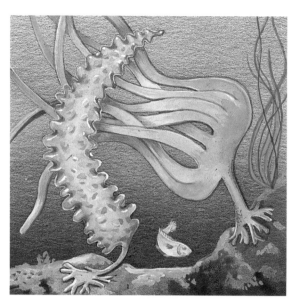

Laminaria clings to a rock with its tendrils.

Wrack floats because of its air-filled pouches called vesicles.

Sea otters live in fields of laminaria. They eat the crustaceans that hide in it. They also float wrapped in seaweed!

HARVESTING WRACK

You can see the wrack harvesters return to port if you visit Brittany. They fish for the big, brown seaweed off the coast called wrack.

Wrack harvesters' ships have articulated arms with a hook at the end made of plaited plastic threads. This hook rips out the seaweed.

The seaweed is loaded onto trucks and delivered to factories. It is used to make different things—ketchup, ice cream and more.

SEA SALT

The sun and wind help the sea water evaporate in salt marshes.
Then all we need to do is gather the salt and sell it.

The water enters the salt marshes through small canals. The salt-marsh workers walk about on the paths that surround the parcels.

This man is collecting the "salt flowers" on the surface of the water.

The salt is carried away in wheelbarrows to be stored.

THE SEAS ARE IN DANGER

Lots of seas, especially landlocked seas, are in danger because of walls of concrete and factories that have "their feet in the water."

Man has destroyed the Aral Sea by turning aside rivers to irrigate fields. The sea does not get new water and is slowly disappearing.

Many dangerous substances are spit into the sea by sewers.

The seas also suffer from the destruction of the coasts that have been marred by concrete.

105

AN OIL PLATFORM

A layer of petrol lies prisoner in between layers of rocks. Men have to dig deeply in order to get it out from under the sea.

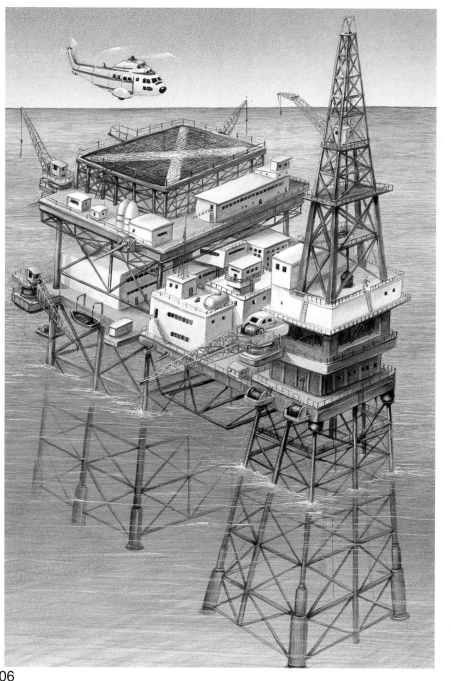

The platform is attached to the sea bottom by solid posts. It will not move even if there is a storm! The mining shaft digs wells in the rock. The oil will come up the shaft to the platform. About one hundred people work on an oil mining platform. They get to and from the platform by helicopter.

BLACK TIDE!

You know that the currents carry everything that floats at sea towards the coasts. When an oil tanker sinks, its oil continues the voyage.

The oil has spread on the sea. It will cover the beaches and rocks at high tide. The tide will be black!

Cleaning beaches is very long, hard work.

This bird is covered in oil and being cleaned with a special soap.

DEAD AND GONE!

Men hunted these animals for food. They killed so many of them that these species have completely disappeared from the planet!

The rhytin lived 300 years ago in the polar waters. It only took 30 years for hunters to kill them all to the very last one.

Whalers and trappers killed the large penguins that lived around the North Pole for their flesh.

ENDANGERED ANIMALS!

These species of animals are in danger. If we continue to hunt them, they will disappear. They must be protected!

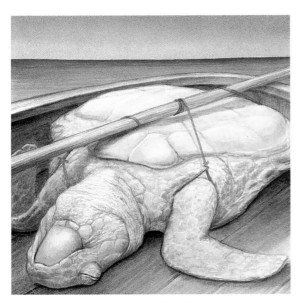

Poachers sell the shells of leatherback turtles.

Hunters kill walruses for their ivory tusks.

There are only 500 monk seals left in the Mediterranean Sea.

Groupers are rare on some shores because they are over-fished.

HUNTING WHALES

Hunters killed 100 whales per day for 50 years. Whaling is now forbidden but some people would like to be allowed to start whaling again!

Fishermen approach whales on a dinghy. They kill them with harpoons and tow them back to the ship.

Whale fat was made into oil for soap and margarine.

The bones were used to make glue and fertilizers.

The whale is pulled up onto the bridge of the ship and cut up right away. Whale meat is a favorite food in many cultures.

PRESERVES FOR THE INHABITANTS OF THE SEA

Fishing and undersea hunting are forbidden in protected areas.
Visitors must respect nature.

Fish multiply rapidly in the undersea preserve in Monaco. They even swim into the hands of divers!

The Bassan gannets' chicks are born and grow in peace in the Sept Iles ("Seven Islands") preserve in Brittany.

WHITE BELUGA WHALES ARE VERY ILL!

These cousins of the dolphins live in the Saint Laurent River in Canada where salt and fresh water mingle.

12,000 factories spit their waste into the river. The fish and beluga whales get all their food from this polluted water.

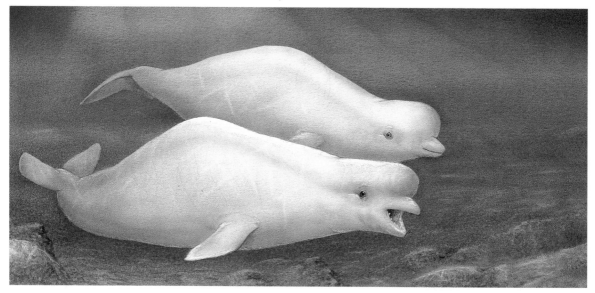

Mother beluga whales swallow dangerous products that get into their milk and poison their babies. Are beluga whales in danger of disappearing?

A CHAIN OF POLLUTION

A shark living in the middle of the ocean can be killed by poisons in the waste of a factory on the edge of a river very far away.

1 – A factory spills its dangerous waste into the river.

2 – The river carries the poison to the sea.

3 – Plankton absorbs the poison.

4 – Herrings eat the sick plankton.

5 – Tuna swallow the poisoned herring.

6 – The tuna— and the poison—reach the shark's stomach.

Dangerous waste has poisoned the entire food chain!

WHAT IF THE EARTH HEATED UP?

The layer of ice that covers the Antarctic continent is so thick that if it melted the level of the oceans would rise!

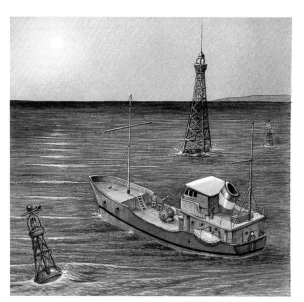 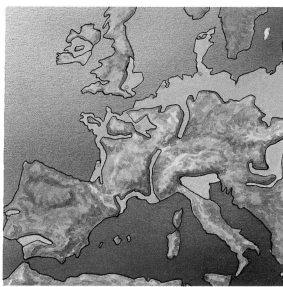

The green areas show the parts of Europe that would disappear under the water. But it would take millions of years for all that ice to melt.

Nothing would change if the icebergs melted! The ice cube in the glass is like an iceberg. The water does not overflow when it melts!

ADVENTURES
AT SEA

THE FIRST DIVERS

Men have always dreamed of visiting the ocean floor. But we had to wait until we figured out how to breathe under water!

Women have long dived for pearl oysters on some Japanese islands without scuba gear. They can hold their breath for several minutes!

This diving suit was the first equipment that let men walk on the ocean floor. The diver was connected to the boat by an air tube.

ON BOARD A SUBMARINE

Most submarines are war ships. Some crews navigate undersea for several months at a time.

periscope

The periscope has to be raised out of the water in order to see what is happening on the surface.

In submarines, sea water is treated in order to provide the oxygen and fresh water needed by the crew.

Submarines fill their ballast tanks with water in order to go down. They push out the water with pressurized air in order to move back up.

SAILS AND OARS

Men first used oars to make ships move forward. Then they learned how to use the wind and built sails.

Vikings were warriors that rode the seas on their longships. These ships had sails and dragon heads. They would row when there was not enough wind.

The Greeks and Romans built the first large warships—galleys. The crews on these ships had to row at a horrendous rhythm.

SAILBOATS TODAY

Today, amateur sailors travel the seas in sailboats. Athletes organize races called regattas.

The Optimist is a small sailboat often used to teach children to sail.

Catamarans are sailboats with two hulls. They race quickly across the waves and can land gently on sandy beaches.

LARGE, BEAUTIFUL SHIPS

In commercial ports you can watch boats come alongside docks and land after their long voyages.

This ocean liner, a hotel ship, is leaving for a wonderful cruise.

The holds of this cargo ship are full of tons of merchandise.

This giant oil tanker has stopped in port to deliver its oil.

Vacationers drive their cars onto this ferry boat.

WHAT GOOD IDEAS!

How can you navigate on frozen polar waters? How can you race at top speed above the waves? Below are two good inventions.

In order to navigate in frozen seas, the front of the icebreaker rests on the ice and breaks it.

The hovercraft transports passengers across short distances. It slides on a cushion of air.

GREAT TRAVELERS OF THE PAST

Christopher Columbus did not know that the Pacific Ocean existed...
but these sailors navigated its waters in simple canoes.

The Maoris used the position of the stars to guide them on their voyages to the islands of the Pacific!

Christopher Columbus, on board his ship, the Santa Maria, discovered the islands close to the American continent.

Magellan died before the end of his long voyage but it was his crew that sailed all the way around the world for the first time.

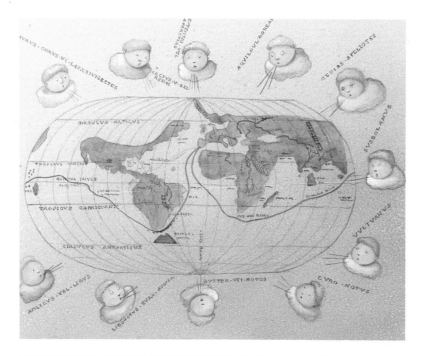

Magellan was the first European to navigate in the Pacific Ocean. The passage between the Atlantic and the Pacific is called the "Strait of Magellan."

Captain Cook made many voyages. He explored the Pacific and discovered Australia. He made other sailors happy by bringing back very valuable maps of the oceans.

ROWING ACROSS THE PACIFIC

The ocean has always called to men and many, many navigators have accomplished feats that are absolutely incredible.

Gérard d'Aboville rowed across the Pacific Ocean in his ship, the Sector. He capsized thirty-six times during the trip!

FINDING YOUR WAY ON THE OCEAN

Navigators have to choose their route and avoid dangers if they want to reach their port. They use instruments that are more and more accurate.

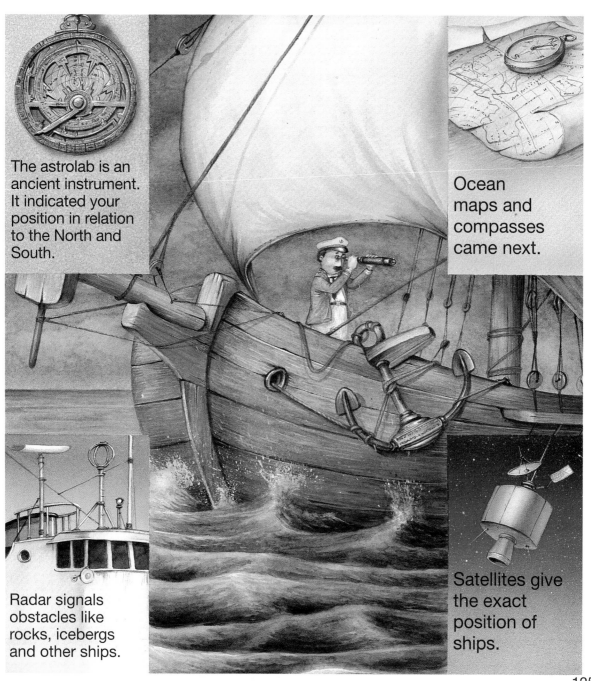

The astrolab is an ancient instrument. It indicated your position in relation to the North and South.

Ocean maps and compasses came next.

Radar signals obstacles like rocks, icebergs and other ships.

Satellites give the exact position of ships.

THE DANGERS OF NAVIGATION

You have to know the maritime code and be very careful when you navigate, even on very big ships!

Cape Horn is a large mass of black rocks against which terrible waves and winds break. It is a nightmare for sailboats!

Radar warns the captain of icebergs so that the ship can navigate through polar waters more easily.

PIRATES AND PRIVATEERS

Pirates, who were high sea bandits, looted ships, and kings paid privateers to capture enemy ships.

Tall ships loaded with precious goods would try and run away whenever the pirates' skull and crossbone flags on pirate ships were spotted!

SHIPWRECKS AND SURVIVORS

Ships sink to the bottom of the sea in shipwrecks. Sunken ships have been resting on the ocean floors ever since they disappeared centuries ago.

The largest ocean liner in the world, the *Titanic*, crashed into an iceberg on its maiden voyage. It lies under 12,000 feet of water!

It is said that dolphins sometimes carry shipwreck victims to the surface so they can breathe and even bring them to shore.

THE SONG OF THE MERMAIDS

Hans Christian Anderson told the story of a nice mermaid. In ancient tales, however, sailors were wary of these fish-women.

Mermaids attracted sailors by singing. But when the sailors left their ships to join them, the mermaids would devour them.

Anderson's little mermaid wants to go to the prince. The witch agrees to give her legs in exchange for her voice!

GIANT MONSTERS

Many legends tell of the adventures of sailors ripped from their ships by giant monsters.

A Swedish writer tells a Scandinavian story of a monster, the Kraken, that looks like a giant octopus.

MOBY DICK

The author of this novel, Herman Melville, sailed often and invented extraordinary stories using what he learned at sea.

Captain Ahab spends his life hunting for Moby Dick, the huge and powerful sperm whale that tore his leg off in a battle.